Published by Barbour Publishing, Inc., P.O. Box 719, Uhrichsville, Ohio 44683
www.barbourbooks.com

 Member of the
Evangelical Christian
Publishers Association

Printed in China.

Baby's
FIRST
CHRISTMAS

Ellyn Sanna

BARBOUR
PUBLISHING, INC.

There's a song in the air!
There's a star in the sky!
There's a mother's deep prayer
And a baby's low cry!

JOSIAH G. HOLLAND, 1879

Congratulations!

There's nothing more wonderful than having a baby in your house at
Christmastime. The presence of this little one will give new depth,
greater happiness, and an even brighter excitement to your holidays.

May you celebrate your baby's first Christmas with joy. . .
may you build precious memories during this special holiday. . .
and may you treasure these memories for a lifetime, allowing them
to deepen your understanding of this holy season.

*A Child is born
in Bethlehem, Bethlehem,
And joy is in Jerusalem.*

LATIN CAROL, 14TH CENTURY

O come, little children, O come, one and all!
O come to the cradle in Bethlehem's stall!
And see what the Father, from high heav'n above,
Has sent us tonight as proof of His love.

CHRISTOPH VON SCHMID, 1768–1854

A Time to Celebrate

Behold, I bring you good tidings of great joy,
which shall be to all people.
For unto you is born this day in the city of David a Saviour,
which is Christ the Lord.

LUKE 2:10–11

Each new child at Christmas reminds our hearts of the Christ Child. As you hold your baby, celebrate the birth of our Savior—and celebrate as well this small new presence in your life. This is a happy time, a time for your family to rejoice together. As you do, the season's celebrations will knit your hearts still closer in love.

On your baby's very first Christmas, no matter how young he is, be sure to include him in the celebrations. He won't remember his first Christmas, but this year is the beginning of a lifetime of traditions and joy. Prepare the way now for Jesus to be born into his life.

Prepare ye the way of the Lord,
make his paths straight.

MARK 1:3

Then let us sing the lullabies of sleep
To this sweet Babe, born to awake us all
From drowsy sin that made old Adam weep,
And by his fault gave to mankind a fall.

For lo! this birth-day, day of days,
Summons our songs, to give him laud and praise.

WILLIAM BYRD 1589

Here are some ways to help your baby enjoy the season's spirit:

- Play Christmas music often. Even the youngest infants will enjoy the soothing sounds of carols. Use Christmas carols as your lullabies when you sing to your baby during the Christmas season.
- Newborns are entranced by the flicker and magic of Christmas tree lights. Set her carrier where she can enjoy the tree.
- If your baby is old enough to grasp objects, allow him to play with an unbreakable nativity set. (Be sure the pieces aren't small enough to fit in his mouth.)
- Make a basket of Christmas cards and look at them with your baby as you would look at picture books. Point to the various nativity animals and name them; repeat the names of Mary and Joseph and the Baby Jesus as you show their pictures to your child.
- Suspend brightly colored Christmas decorations from your ceilings and lamps. Place them where your child can look up and watch them dangle in the air.
- Make a Christmas mobile to hang above her crib. (Directions are on page 12.)

Once in royal David's city
Stood a lowly cattle shed,
Where a mother laid her Baby
In a manger for His bed:
Mary was that mother mild,
Jesus Christ, her little Child.

For He is our childhood's pattern;
Day by day like us He grew;
He was little, weak and helpless,
Tears and smiles like us He knew;
And He feeleth for our sadness,
And He shareth in our gladness.

CECIL F. ALEXANDER, 1848

Christmas Mobile for Baby

You will need:

* 2 or 3 eight-inch long dowels with ¼-inch diameters (or use twigs for a more rustic look)
* red and/or green ¼-inch ribbon
* an assortment of brightly colored Christmas objects. For instance:

Candy canes
Bells
Shiny ball decorations
Small stuffed sheep, donkeys, or camels
Stars
Gingerbread people
Angels

Tie the dowels or sticks together with 6-inch lengths of ribbon. Use various lengths of ribbon (from 3 inches to 8 inches) to attach your collection of objects to the sticks. Make sure they balance each other. On the top dowel, tie a length of ribbon long enough to attach the mobile from the ceiling. (Or, if your baby already has a crib mobile, remove the hanging part and replace with your homemade mobile.) Be sure the mobile is high enough that your baby will not be able to grasp it.

Enjoy watching as your child is entranced by the dancing Christmas display above her head!

Make sure your baby's first Christmas is a safe and happy one. Here are some safety precautions to keep in mind during your celebrations:

* If your child is crawling, make sure you have child protectors in all outlets and extension cords that are not being used.
* Hang only unbreakable decorations on the lowest branches of your tree.
* Consider putting your tree inside a playpen or on a table if your child is prone to pulling things over.
* Make sure poinsettias and other holiday plants are not left where Baby can grab and eat.
* Never place your child's carrier near lit candles.
* Keep small decorations that could be swallowed out of Baby's reach.

And whoso shall receive one such little child

in my name receiveth me.

MATTHEW 18:5

Christmas a is special holiday, like none other,
because at the very center of all the celebration is a baby.
We are used to thinking of God as mighty, powerful,
omnipotent—and yet at Christmas,
the Son of God became a tiny, human infant,
as helpless and vulnerable, as precious and perfect as your baby.

And a little child shall lead them.

ISAIAH 11:6

Can we see the little Child,
Is He within?
If we lift the wooden latch
May we go in?

Great kings have precious gifts,
And we have nought,
Little smiles and little tears
Are all we brought.

FRANCES CHESTERTON

A Time to Remember

Silent night! Holy night! All is calm, all is bright,
Round yon virgin mother and Child.
Holy Infant, so tender and mild,
Sleep in heavenly peace!

JOSEPH MOHR, 1818

Mary kept all these things,
and pondered them in her heart.

LUKE 2:19

Think what memories Mary must have had of that first Christmas! Because she shared her memories with Luke, the Gospel author, we have a deeper understanding of her Son's birth.

Your baby won't remember her very first Christmas—but you will. This is a special season in your life and in the life of your baby. Gather your memories together. One day they may help your child understand a little better the meaning and value of her own life.

What Child is this, who laid to rest
On Mary's lap, is sleeping?
Whom angels greet with anthems sweet,
While shepherds watch are keeping?
This, this is Christ the King,
Whom shepherds guard and angels sing:
Haste, haste to bring Him laud,
The Babe, the Son of Mary.

WILLIAM CHATTERTON DIX, 1837–1898

On your baby's first Christmas. . .

Length: _____

Weight: _____

New achievements:_____

_____

_____

_____

_____

_____

_____

_____

_____

_____

_____

Come and look upon the Child,
Nestling in the hay!
See His fair arms opened wide,
On her lap to play!
Little angels all around
Danced, and carols flung;
Making verselets sweet and true,
Still of love they sung;
Calling saints and sinners too
With love's tender tongue;
Now that heaven's high glory is
On this earth displayed.

JACOPONE OF TODI (1230),
TRANSLATED BY JOHN ADDINGTON SYMONDS

My baby's favorite gifts:

_____ from _____
_____ from _____
_____ from _____
_____ from _____
_____ from _____
_____ from _____
_____ from _____
_____ from _____
_____ from _____
_____ from _____
_____ from _____
_____ from _____
_____ from _____
_____ from _____
_____ from _____
_____ from _____
_____ from _____

Away in a manger, no crib for a bed,
The little Lord Jesus lay down His sweet head.
The stars in the sky look'd down where He lay,
The little Lord Jesus, asleep in the hay.

Be near me, Lord Jesus, I ask Thee to stay
Close by me forever and love me, I pray!
Bless all the dear children in Thy tender care,
And take us to heaven, to live with Thee there.

AMERICAN CAROL, 19TH CENTURY

Handprint Christmas Decoration

Make a decoration to hang on your tree that will always remind you of this special Christmas.

You will need:

* plaster of Paris from a craft store
* large lid from a peanut butter or pickle jar (about 4-inch diameter)
* spray varnish
* ribbon
* lace, ribbon, or rickrack
* glue

Follow the directions for mixing the plaster of Paris. Lubricate the lid with liquid soap or shortening and then fill with the wet plaster. While the plaster is still soft, press your baby's hand into it to make a deep, clear print. Write the date and your baby's name in the soft plaster with a knife or the point of a pen. Poke a straw through the plaster above your baby's handprint to create a hole for hanging.

When the plaster is dry, gently tap it out of the lid. To preserve and strengthen the plaster, spray it with varnish. When the varnish is dry, decorate the circle with colored lace, ribbon, or rickrack. Hang with a ribbon through the hole.

To create colored plaster, add one package of Rit dye to one quart of hot water. Mix 4 ounces or ½ cup of dye to each pound of dry plaster.

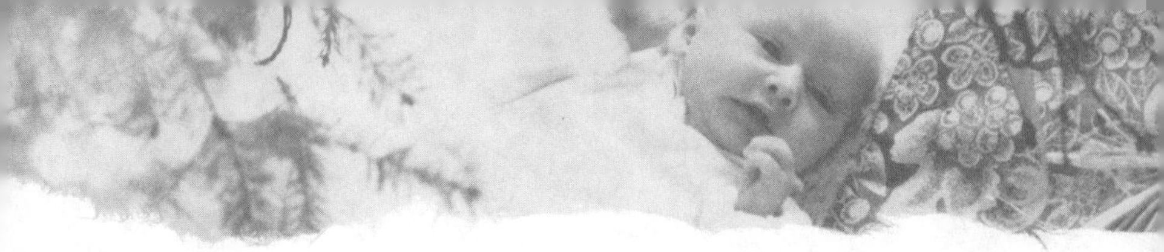

My favorite memory from my baby's first Christmas was

_____

_____

_____

_____

_____

_____

_____

_____

_____

_____

_____

_____

When my baby is older, I would like to share these thoughts about the first Christmas we had together:

_____

_____

_____

_____

_____

_____

_____

_____

_____

_____

_____

Use these pages for photos from your baby's first Christmas.

BABY'S FIRST CHRISTMAS

Given, not lent,
And not withdrawn, once sent,
This Infant of mankind, this One,
Is still the little welcome Son.
New every year,
New-born and newly dear,
He comes with tidings and a song,
The ages long, the ages long.

ALICE MAYNELL

A Time to Treasure

Rock-a-bye, Jesus, my soul's fairest treasure,
Rock-a-bye, Jesus, my love knows no measure.
Rock-a-bye, Jesus sweet, close I will hold Thee, I'll hold Thee,
As Mary's loving arms did enfold Thee.

POLISH CAROL

Great little one! whose all-embracing birth
Lifts earth to heaven, stoops heaven to earth.

RICHARD CRASHAW, 1613–1649

As you treasure the memories of your baby's first Christmas, you'll find that your own heart is changed and deepened by this joyous time. Open yourself to the reminders of the Christ Child you see in the wonder of your own baby. Lift your heart from earth to heaven, knowing that God's heart is reaching down to you.

And know as well that God delights with you as you enjoy your child. Rest in the knowledge that He treasures your child far more even than you do.

The darkness is falling, the day is nigh gone.

I come to adore Thee, the heavenly Son.

I sing by Thy cradle a sweet lullaby.

Thou art not yet sleeping, I hear Thy soft cry.

Bye, bye, bye, sleep sweet, dearest Child.

AUSTRIAN CAROL

Lullabies for Jesus

Down through the ages, people around the world have been touched by the thought of God coming to us as a baby. The lullabies that have been written for the Christ Child, like the ones included in this section, show that every culture must have thought of the Baby Jesus as they rocked their own babies to sleep.

As you hold your baby during this special season, allow these thoughts to deepen your love. Treasure the reflection of Jesus you see in your baby's eyes. Sing your own love songs to your baby—and to the Lord who loves you both.

He who heaven created,
Lully, lully, lu,
Born is He in stable stall,
Bye, bye, bye.
He the King who ruleth all,
Lully, lully, lu.

Joseph he bought the swaddling clothes,
Lully, lully, lu,
Mary the mother kind and mild,
Bye, bye, bye,
Into the crib she put the Child,
Lully, lully, lu.

ENGLISH CAROL, 15TH CENTURY

A la ru-ru-ru, my Baby dearest,
O sleep, my Jesus, sleep, my fairest.
From elephant to flies that creep, no noise before Him,
Your silence keep, we all shall now adore Him.
A la ru-ru-ru, my Baby dearest, O sleep, my Jesus, sleep my fairest.

MEXICAN CAROL

Little Jesus, sweetly sleep, do not stir;
We will lend a coat of fur.
We will rock You, rock You, rock You,
See the fur to keep You warm,
Snugly round Your tiny form.

CZECH CAROL

Lullaby and good night!
With angels in sight;
For you'll surely see
Baby Jesus' Christmas tree.
Sleep then, resting in peace,
Dream of Paradise sweet;
Sleep then, resting in peace,
Dream of Paradise sweet.

JOHANNES BRAHMS, 1833–1897,
TRANSLATED BY ARTHUR WESTBROOK

As parents, when we hold our babies in our arms, we can't help but be struck by their total and absolute vulnerability. Human newborns are overwhelmingly, awesomely dependent on their parents for care. Our responsibility to them is intensely sweet—and yet terribly frightening.

Imagine, then, how Mary must have felt as she held the Creator of the universe, wrapped in swaddling clothes. How did God dare to send His only Son to us in such a terrifyingly fragile package?

Only love could have risked so much. That same love is present in your home this year at Christmas.

And the Word was made flesh, and dwelt among us.

JOHN 1:14

And the child grew, and waxed strong in spirit,
filled with wisdom:
and the grace of God was upon him.

LUKE 2:40

Dear Lord,
May this child's first Christmas be blessed by You. Although she is too young to understand yet, may she grow to know the richness of Your love. May she, like Jesus, grow strong in spirit and be filled with wisdom. May Your grace be always with her.

Amen.